EPICMEALTIME

THE COLLECTOR'S COOKBOOK

HARLEY MORENSTEIN
AND JOSH ELKIN

GALLERY BOOKS

New York   London   Toronto   Sydney   New Delhi

G

Gallery Books
A Division of Simon & Schuster, Inc.
1230 Avenue of the Americas
New York, NY 10020

Copyright © 2014 by NextTime Productions, Ltd.

First Gallery Books trade paperback edition March 2014

GALLERY BOOKS and colophon are registered trademarks of Simon & Schuster, Inc.

For information about special discounts for bulk purchases, please contact Simon & Schuster Special Sales at 1-866-506-1949 or business@simonandschuster.com.

The Simon & Schuster Speakers Bureau can bring authors to your live event. For more information or to book an event contact the Simon & Schuster Speakers Bureau at 1-866-248-3049 or visit our website at www.simonspeakers.com.

Photography: Daniel Nguyen
Assistant: Clay Boonthanakit
Bio Photos: Marlon Kuhnreich
Design and Layout: Fancy Boys
Illustration (pages 60–61): Azad Injejikian

Manufactured in the United States of America

10 9 8 7 6 5 4 3 2 1

Library of Congress Cataloging-in-Publication Data is available.

ISBN 978-1-4767-4601-2
ISBN 978-1-4767-4602-9 (ebook)

Table of Contents

The best way to read this book is straight through, player. Then come back to it as reference material every day until you learn this shit.

CBH

Cox, Bullock & Haneous

44 Old Bell End, Crooksby, SE11 0UT, England

Dear EpicMealTime

I'm writing on behalf of my client Jamie Oliver: chef, author and world-renowned healthy food campaigner.

Mr Oliver has informed me that you've been harassing him to write a foreword for your up-and-coming EpicMealTime cookbook. He wishes you and your team good luck, but cannot endorse any of the recipes as it simply goes against everything he believes in. Your conduct and style of cooking is not only repulsive, disgusting and against all good English table manners, but your gross overconsumption of highly processed, low-quality junk food can only be a bad thing for the environment, small local businesses and the health of any person mad enough to venture within spitting distance of you crazy Canadian fellows.

Although he does agree that adding more bacon to pretty much anything makes it taste better, he hopes that no one partakes in eating any of the food featured in your book, as it would seriously damage their health. Please stop calling, writing and emailing Mr Oliver, and stop posting the leftovers to his house after filming or I will be forced to take further action with the local law enforcement, i.e. back off or we'll sue your ass.

Yours sincerely

Boris Bullock
Legal Director
Cox, Bullock & Haneous

Jamie Oliver
Chef and Author
Jamie Oliver Limited

SAUCE BOSS

HARLEY MORENSTEIN

FIRST EPISODE: Fast Food Pizza
EATING STYLE: Calculated
POSITION: Grand Admiral Master Chief/Commander General

The fuckin' brains of *EpicMealTime*, the hairy face of *EpicMealTime*, and of course, the booming voice of *EpicMealTime*; Harley Morenstein, a.k.a. Sauce Boss! Harley was a schoolteacher until the summer of 2010, when he created *EpicMealTime* in his backyard. Harley went from schooling noobs to snuggling boobs in just a few months. With no editing skills and no camera training, he bought a fuckin' laptop (balling) and a camera (boss balling) on a teacher's salary (not balling) and taught himself how to produce a show. *Big-time moves right there*. Although *EpicMealTime* started out as a hobby, Harley became seriously commited to producing a legit series. The first 60+ videos of *EpicMealTime* were single-handedly edited by the Sauce Boss himself. *What you know about video-editing software?* Although he touches the food on the rarest of occasions, he takes no part in the cooking. Fuck that, he's got a good goon squad to handle that shit. All of the meals come from his mind and are passed down to the rest of the team, who further mutate them. Finally, each meal is filtered back through the "Brain" of the Sauce Boss to ensure maximum Next-Level Intelligence of the Epic Meal.

WHAT YOU DON'T KNOW

Egg beating! More than 15 dozen (that's 180 for you dumbasses) chicks have been fingered on *EpicMealTime*.

"WHAT YOU KNOW ABOUT COOKING?"

WORST PIZZA

INGREDIENTS

1 large cheese pizza

1 Crunch Wrap Supreme (Taco Bell)

1 large French fries (Wendy's)

1 large order popcorn chicken (KFC)

6 McNuggets

1 Big Mac

1 Baconator (Wendy's)

1 Teen Burger (A&W)

2 orders onion rings (A&W)

2 16-ounce bags grated mozzarella cheese

SERVES: *2 men or 4 little bitches*

TOTAL CALORIES
5 1 2 1

Step 3

Step 5

Step 7

Step 9

EQUIPMENT

1 large cookie sheet or piece of tinfoil made into baking sheet apparatus

1 pizza cutter

DIRECTIONS

1. Preheat the oven to 350°F.

2. Lay cheese pizza on baking sheet or tinfoil baking apparatus.

3. Start by decorating pizza with Crunch Wrap Supreme in the middle of the pie, using it as a guide to decorate the rest.

4. Recklessly sprinkle half the French fries and all the popcorn chicken and nuggets around the perimeter of the Crunch Wrap Supreme.

5. Place the Big Mac, Baconator, and Teen Burger around the pizza in a triangle, using the Crunch Wrap as a midpoint.

6. Finally, sprinkle the remaining French fries and the A&W onion rings around the entire pie.

7. Pour as much mozzarella cheese onto the pizza as you can.

8. Put into oven for 12 minutes or until the cheese is bubbling.

9. Take pizza out of the oven and let sit to cool down. Once the pizza isn't super hot, cut with pizza cutter and let the clogging of the arteries begin.

ANGRY FRENCH CANADIAN

INGREDIENTS

1 pound bacon

6 eggs

1 20-inch French baguette

1 16-ounce can maple syrup

1½ large orders poutine (French fries drenched with gravy and topped with cheese curds or mozzarella cheese)

3 steamed hot dogs with buns

No cast member of *EpicMealTime* has any culinary education or previous professional cooking experience.

SERVES: *1 Muscles Glasses or 3 humans or 5 little hater bitches*

TOTAL CALORIES

3661

Step 1

Step 4

Step 8

Step 9

EQUIPMENT

1 large bowl for egg wash

1 frying pan

DIRECTIONS

1. Fry up all the bacon and let sit on the side.

2. Crack eggs into large bowl and beat for dunking.

3. Slice the baguette in half.

4. Cut the baguette halves into thirds in order to fit in the pan, then dunk the inside cut slice of bread into the egg wash.

5. Fry the pieces of baguette until golden on egg side.

6. Place the bread on a large plate and pour maple syrup over all 6 pieces.

7. Lay the bacon on 3 pieces of bread.

8. Put the poutine over all the bacon, covering the beast.

9. Take the steamed hot dogs with buns and place one on each poutine-covered piece of bread.

10. Attempt to close sandwiches and drench them in the remaining maple syrup.

The Angry French Canadian should weigh about 4 to 5 pounds (per 1/3), depending on whether you work in a shipping facility or if you just work out a lot.

THE DOUBLE KILL

INGREDIENTS

1 pound bacon   *Don't fuck around with burgers!*

4 beef burgers

1 liter vegetable oil

4 boneless chicken breasts

1 white onion

6 eggs

1 32-ounce container bread crumbs

4 cups all-purpose flour

1 box mac 'n cheese

1 32-ounce pack sliced cheddar cheese

4 hamburger buns

SERVES: *1 person . . . unless your balls haven't dropped yet!*

TOTAL CALORIES
2700

EQUIPMENT

1 deep-dish (3 inches or more deep) skillet

3 deep bowls for egg wash, flour, and bread crumbs

1 pair of tongs (for grip)

1 pack of extra-long skewers

2 sheets of plastic wrap

DIRECTIONS

1. Throw the bacon into the hot skillet or frying pan. Cook it to *EMT* level four on the bacon-meter. Empty the bacon grease into a glass bottle every time you reload the pan with fresh bacon. When it's done, chuck it to the side with some paper towels over it. Remember to NOT clean the pan after the bacon is cooked. You want all the flavor you can get for the burgers.

2. Take that hot, bacon-greased pan, set the burner in between medium and high heat, and throw on the hamburgers. Once they're cooked, throw them to the side, and cover them with foil to keep warm.

3. Let the pan cool down and fill it with vegetable oil (1 inch) and heat to about 375°F.

4. While the oil is heating up, take the chicken breasts out (remember, keep your hands clean when dealing with raw chicken; no one needs to experience salmonella poisoning). Lay out a piece of plastic wrap and put a chicken breast on top. Take another piece of plastic wrap and put it on top of the chicken. Proceed to beat the chicken until ultra thin. Repeat with the remaining breasts. Put the chicken to the side on a plate.

5. Cut the onion in half, then into slices, separating the the slices into rings.

6. Crack the eggs into one bowl and beat them. Place bread crumbs in the second bowl and flour in the third bowl. You should have a bowl of beaten eggs, a bowl of flour, and a bowl of bread crumbs.

7. Take raw onion rings and throw them into the bowl of beaten eggs. Cover them thoroughly. Then throw them into the flour (cover them again), and then back into the egg wash. Then, get those onions into the bread crumbs for a final coating. Once breaded, put the onions on a plate and into the fridge.

8. If the current dipping bowls are not full enough, add some more of each ingredient to the corresponding bowl to repeat this breading procedure with the beaten chicken.

9. Drench chicken breast with egg. Then throw the chicken into the flour and then back into the egg. Cover with egg, and then throw into the bread crumbs. Repeat with remaining breasts. Each time you're done handling the chicken, wash your hands with soap and water.

10. It's time to fry up the onions and chicken. Carefully put a breaded chicken breast into the hot vegetable oil using the tongs. The idea is to get each side of the chicken dark golden brown (frying about 2 minutes on each side). Repeat with the remaining breasts.

11. Do the same thing with the onions that you did with the chicken. This time, flip the onions after 45 seconds on each side, or when golden brown.

WHAT YOUR MOM KNOWS AND YOU DON'T

Blood is thicker than water; bacon grease is thicker than blood; blood and bacon grease make a fantastic energy drink.

Step 4

12. Heat a pot of water for the mac 'n cheese. Cook it up the way you normally would. (directions are usually on the box.)

13. Toasting the buns is the last step before . . . ASSEMBLY TIME.

Step 11

14. Start by laying out a piece of fried chicken then mac 'n cheese then bacon then chicken then cheese then bun then burger then cheese then burger then bacon then mac 'n cheese then bun then onion then cheese then bun then burger then bacon then cheese then onion then burger then bun then bacon then mac 'n cheese then chicken then cheese then mac 'n cheese and then chicken. Put the skewers through the entire Double Kill for eating support.

Step 14

ATTACK

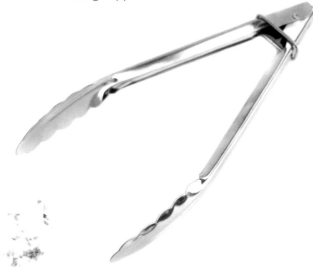

MUSCLES GLASSES

FIRST EPISODE: Fast Food Pizza
EATING STYLE: Demolition
POSITION: Heavyweight Champion

IF YOU DON'T KNOW, NOW YOU KNOW

EMT also stands for "Emergency Medical Technician"—now that's a fucking LOL!

"TASTES LIKE CRAZY ALCOHOL RAINBOW PIG"

TRIPLE MEAT LOG

INGREDIENTS

3 liters vegetable oil

1½ pounds bacon or 18 slices

3 large hot dogs

1½ pounds ground meat trifecta
(beef/pork/veal)

2 eggs

1 cup bread crumbs

+ Salt and pepper

1 large brick cheddar cheese

2 egg yolks

1 cup reserved bacon grease

+ Dijon mustard

3 cups all purpose flour

1½ cups yellow cornmeal

3 tablespoons sugar

4½ teaspoons baking powder

1 teaspoon salt

2 cups buttermilk

*Eaten like a typical corn dog, it's good for
1 person. If you're cutting it into slices like
bread, it's good for 4 people.*

SERVES:

TOTAL CALORIES

5 8 2 6

WHAT YOU DON'T KNOW

Some might say the first *EpicMeal-Time* video is on Harley's old YouTube channel. The video features him eating a 6-patty burger with 18 strips of bacon.

EQUIPMENT

1 deep fryer or large soup pot

1 frying pan

1 blender

1 large wooden spoon

+ plastic wrap

+ tinfoil

1 baking sheet

DIRECTIONS

THE MEAT

A1. Preheat the oven to 395°F.

A2. Put vegetable oil in deep fryer and preheat to 375°F.

A3. Fry up all those bacon strips. After every batch, pour the bacon grease into a glass bowl for mayonnaise (for best-tasting mayo, leave bacon fragments in the extracted grease).

A4. Cook the hot dogs.

* Put the hot dogs and bacon aside for later.

A5. Take out the ground meat and throw it into a bowl. Add eggs and then bread crumbs. Season with salt and pepper, and mix it up. Don't be a bitch, use your hands.

THE LOG

Step B3

B1. Use the plastic wrap as a base for the meat blanket. Spread the meat an inch away from the border on each side. The blanket should be about ¼ inch thick.

* The idea is to wrap the hot dogs in the blanket. If your hot dogs are small, adjust the size of the blanket accordingly.

B2. Slice the entire brick of cheddar cheese.

Step B3

B3. Starting laying the bacon strips an inch from the top of the blanket. Add the cheddar cheese in the same direction as the bacon. Finish off the first step of the meat blanket by making a hot dog pyramid in the horizontal direction of the meat blanket. The hot dog pyramid should be in the middle of the bacon-cheddar layers.

B4. Use the plastic wrap to start the rolling process. Use the side where you left an inch of bare meat. Start rolling the meat (always holding onto the plastic wrap). The first roll of the meat log should cover one side of the hot dog pyramid. Then roll tight using the plastic wrap to tighten every turn. Twist the plastic wrap on each end of the log as tight as you can. This will tighten the log as well. Put the log in the fridge for 10 minutes.

Step B6

B5. Time to make the bacon mayo. Add the egg yolks to the blender. Use the 1 cup of bacon grease and put it in with the eggs. Add 1 tablespoon of Dijon mustard or more, depending on your desired tartness, and then start blending until the mixture reaches a mayo-like consistency.

B6. Once the bacon mayo is done, put it in the fridge and take out the settled meat log. Take off the plastic wrap and rewrap the meat log in tinfoil. Put it on a baking sheet and into the oven for 30 minutes or until cooked through.

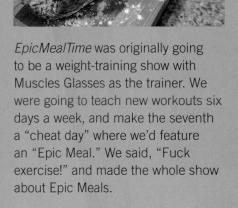

EpicMealTime was originally going to be a weight-training show with Muscles Glasses as the trainer. We were going to teach new workouts six days a week, and make the seventh a "cheat day" where we'd feature an "Epic Meal." We said, "Fuck exercise!" and made the whole show about Epic Meals.

DEEP FRYING

C1. Sift the flour, cornmeal, sugar, baking powder, and salt into a bowl. Add the buttermilk and whisk. Batter is done when a spoon can stand up in middle of the mixture.

C2. Once the meat log is fully cooked, let it rest until room temperature. When it's cooled, cover the entire thing in the buttermilk batter.

** CAUTION ** Please be advised that *EpicMealTime* chefs have superhuman strength regarding high heat. Take extra precaution while dunking this monstrosity in hot oil.

C3. Dunk the fully covered meat log into the hot oil until golden brown. Take out and let sit for 5 minutes.

C4. Go get your bacon mayo and a super-hot chick, and enjoy while your meat log gets devoured.

TURBACON EPIC

INGREDIENTS

1 medium-sized pig—preferably dead

+ dry rub

5 pounds sausage meat (cut-open sausage links if you can't find meat). This is important, as it is your "meat glue"!!

7 packs bacon!

1 dozen butter croissants.
Don't fuck around with the pronunciation.

1 each medium-sized turkey, chicken, duck, Cornish hen, and quail, all deboned and butterflied. Fuck the avian race!! amirite?!

3–4 sticks butter

1 2-liter bottle Dr Pepper. We use Dr Pepper but you can use whatever the fuck you want!

6 Wendy's Baconators (for garnish). Garnish it with Baconators?! We did, 'cause we were fuckin' stoned!

+ brown sugar

EQUIPMENT

1 BBQ smoker (or Google how to turn a regular BBQ into a smoker)

1 cooking twine and needle

1 frying pan

+ metal trays

Even if you are a Muscles Glasses, invite the whole family over for this badass culinary fucker of mothers!

SERVES:

TOTAL CALORIES

79046

WHAT YOUR MOM KNOWS

Archiving shit!! There is 1TB of bacon-flipping footage on *EpicMealTime* that hasn't been used.

DIRECTIONS

*Prep the pig and let it sit while you prepare the birds.

PREPPING THE PIG

A1. Prep the pig by throwing on your favorite mix of dry rub. Any flavor will do; we used bacon salt.

MEAT GLUE

B1. Take sausages out of casings and place in a bowl. Mix and knead the sausage until it reaches a somewhat sticky consistency.

BACON-CROISSANT STUFFING

C1. Chop up 5 packs of bacon and throw it in a pan.

C2. Melt a stick of butter and set aside.

C3. When the bacon gets somewhat crisp, drain 90% of the bacon grease and add the butter and half of the croissants (chopped).

C4. Mix well and then add the remaining croissants.

C5. When the stuffing is well mixed, remove and place in a bowl.

ASSEMBLING THE BIRDS

D1. Lay out the turkey with the skinside down.

D2. Apply the meat glue on top of the turkey.

D3. Add some stuffing.

D4. On top of the stuffing, add the duck and then some more meat glue.

D5. Cover the entire duck with bacon strips.

D6. Add more meat glue.

D7. Put the chicken on top, then apply more meat glue.

D8. Put the hen on top, then add more meat glue.

D9. Fold one half of the bird pile onto the other half (be careful that the insides don't fall out).

D10. Use the turkey to hold all the birds together.

D11. Start threading the turkey. Use cooking twine and a needle.

D12. You don't have to thread through all the birds; if you thread through the turkey it will work just fine. You might need someone to help you hold the whole thing together. Start at the top of the turkey and work your way down the entire structure until all the birds are together.

D13. Put the birds in a metal dish seam-side down and lay bacon strips over the top.

D14. Add brown sugar for some intense flavor.

D15. The oven should be set to 375°F. Cook the birds for 45 minutes. Then remove and let stand for 30 minutes.

STUFFING THE PIG

E1. Place the birds inside the pig stomach. Use the remaining bacon-croissant stuffing to fill the gaps of the pig's stomach. At this point you will need some assistance to close the pig stomach. Sew the pig closed and prepare to throw it on the smoker. We recommend using a thicker twine, because pig skin is tougher than bird skin.

COOKING THE PIG

F1. Cook the pig on the smoker according to its size and weight. Use a meat thermometer to determine whether it's fully cooked. Halfway through, you should add bacon strips as armor.

DR PEPPER BUTTER-BASTING SAUCE

G1. Pour the Dr Pepper into a pot.

G2. Add 2 sticks of butter and heat until combined. Use this mixture to baste the pig every 45 minutes. If you run out, make more.

G3. Now garnish pig with the Baconators and serve it to your family or a whole bunch of bacon-horny sluts!

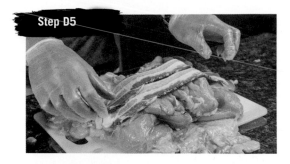

Step D5

Step D11

Step D13

Step D14

TOTAL CALORIES
18531

BREAKFAST OF BOOZE

INGREDIENTS

+ cinnamon and brown sugar

3–4 pounds bacon

2 boxes pancake mix

+ beer

1 small precooked deli ham

1 tenderloin steak

1 box breakfast sausages

4–5 jalapeño peppers

+ cream cheese

+ chocolate chips

1 5-pound bag potatoes (Yukon Gold will work)

12 eggs

1 carton heavy whipping cream

1 bottle Baileys Irish Cream

1 loaf white bread

+ butter

2 cups all-purpose flour

1 bag Doritos Original

1 bag cheese sticks

2 gallons cooking oil (for deep frying)

2 cans maple syrup

1 large bottle whiskey

EQUIPMENT

1 baking sheet

1 large pot or deep fryer

1 large, oven-friendly pan

1 waffle maker

1 grater

+ tinfoil

This was a special episode as it was the first time we fully incorporated liquor into a meal! Don't fuck around, make sure you get drunk before, during, and after eating these pancakes!

Step C1

Step E1

Step J2

Step J5

DIRECTIONS

CANDY BACON

A1. Preheat the oven to 375°F.

A2. In a bowl, mix two parts brown sugar with one part cinnamon.

A3. Lay out a pound of bacon strips on a baking sheet covered in tinfoil so that the sides of the strips aren't touching.

A4. Sprinkle the cinnamon-sugar mixture over all the bacon strips.

A5. Bake until the mixture starts bubbling.

A6. Take out the candy bacon and flip that shit. Then apply more sugar mixture.

A7. Bake until bubbling.

A8. Once fully cooked, transfer candy bacon strips to fresh tinfoil and place in the fridge to harden.

REGULAR BACON

B1. Cover a cookie sheet in tinfoil.

B2. Lay bacon strips across the sheet.

B3. Cook remaining bacon, setting aside a few strips.

DEEP-FRY BATTER

C1. To be efficient, use a dry pancake mix and add beer. (As much as you like!)

C2. Place into a large bowl and save for various items.

DEEP-FRIED BACON-WRAPPED SLICED HAM

D1. Slice ham into ¼-inch pieces.

D2. Wrap bacon around ham in the shape of a cross.

D3. Use skewers to secure the bacon onto the ham and to add support for battering and deep-frying.

D4. Dip the bacon-wrapped ham into the batter, and deep fry until light gold and crispy.

DEEP-FRIED STEAK

E1. Cut steak lengthwise into inch-thick pieces.

E2. Dip into deep-fry batter.

E3. Deep fry until light gold and crispy.

DEEP-FRIED CREAM CHEESE JALAPEÑO PANCAKE

F1. Heat up a pan and make large pancakes using prepared beer batter.

F2. Once the pancakes are done, use the same pan to fry up some sausage.

F3. Chop the jalapeños and remove the seeds. (If you want them really spicy, you can leave the seeds in.)

F4. Lay one pancake out on a plate. Spread some cream cheese in the middle. Place a sausage on top of the cream cheese and sprinkle with jalapeños.

F5. Fold the pancake toward the middle of the sausage/jalapeño–cream cheese mix.

F6. Use skewers to secure it in place and slather with deep fry batter.

F7. Deep fry until lightly golden-brown and crispy.

CHOCOLATE CHIP BACON WAFFLES

G1. Preheat waffle maker to medium-high.

G2. Add batter and begin to cook.

G3. When bubbles begin to form on the surface, add crushed bacon and chocolate chips.

G4. Continue process until waffle is fully cooked.

Serve with maple syrup and whiskey.

WHAT YOU ONLY WISH YOU KNEW

When the *EpicMealTime* team flies, they always sit in the emergency exit row because all pilots have the utmost respect and trust in them.

HASH BROWN BALLS

H1. Shred potatoes using a grater.

H2. Put potatoes in a pot and add one egg yolk per cup of shredded potatoes. Season with salt and pepper.

H3. Use your hands to roll the mixture into little balls. Then immerse these balls in 375°F cooking oil.

H4. Repeat until all of balls have been deep-fried.

BAILEYS WHIPPED CREAM

I1. Take a few of the already cooked bacon strips and put them back in the 375°F oven for 10 minutes.

I2. Pour the whipping cream into a bowl. Whisk vigorously.

I3. Once the cream stiffens just a little, add some Baileys to taste.

I4. Continue beating the cream and Baileys until you create soft peaks of cream.

I5. Finally, crush up the overcooked bacon, and add it to the whipped cream mixture.

BACON CREAM CHEESE– STUFFED FRENCH TOAST

J1. Cut the crusts off 25 slices of white bread.

J2. Place a dollop of cream cheese and a few slices of bacon in the center of one piece of bread, then cover with another slice.

J3. Use a fork to press down on the edges of the two pieces of bread to ensure they stay sandwiched together.

J4. Crack a few eggs into a bowl to be used as coating for the French toast. Beat eggs.

J5. Heat up a pan, add some butter, and fry up some French toast until golden brown on each side.

J6. Repeat until you've done all the pockets of goodness.

DEEP-FRIED DORITO CHEESE STICKS

K1. Put the flour in a bowl.

K2. In a separate bowl crack and beat a few eggs for an egg wash.

K3. Smash a few handfuls of Doritos in another bowl.

K4. Coat each cheese stick with flour, then egg wash, then crushed Doritos.

K5. Immerse in pot of 375°F oil and deep-fry for 15 seconds per stick.

BUILDING

L1. Throw all of this together into a castle-like creation. Don't fuck around, 'cause this is the fortress that will keep the haters out! You don't want any of them haters near your shit, do you?

TYLER!

TYLER LEMCO

First Episode: Double Kill
Last Episode: Meat Cake
Eating Style: Face Dive
Position: Scientist/Data Analyst

Some would say Tyler! is "special"; others would agree. Most people would agree, actually. This is because Tyler! is a number-crunching part-time rapper and the only scientist who wears a gold donkey rope. The fact that Tyler! gained more weight when he was on the team than anyone else was truly a testament to his dedication to the movement that is *EpicMealTime*. If you have any "special" friends, just know this: Tyler! is our special friend and he can stomp the shit out of your special friend. Even though a lot of his weight was gained off-camera, Tyler! did employ creativity while eating on-camera. He also likes to play with toys in the swimming pool!

IF YOU DON'T KNOW, NOW YOU KNOW

Not one member of the *EpicMealTime* team is lactose intolerant.

"THAT BITE HURT MY JAW"

FAST FOOD SUSHI

INGREDIENTS

1 pound bacon, cooked

1 pound bacon, uncooked

2 Big Macs

4 large orders French fries (McDonalds')

9 Chicken McNuggets

2 Crunch Wrap Supremes (Taco Bell)

1 order French Fries Supreme (Taco Bell)

1 large order popcorn chicken (KFC)

+ Cole slaw / gravy (KFC)

+ Sauces: Gather all the sauces you can think of

EQUIPMENT

1 sushi roller

1 baking sheet

+ tinfoil

SERVES: *1 Muscles Glasses, 2 human beings, or 4 whiny losers*

TOTAL CALORIES

11816

Step A1

Step A3

Step B1

Step D1

DIRECTIONS

BACON SUSHI ROLL

A1. Before laying out all your fast food, prepare your bacon wraps a.k.a. bacon sushi roll. Lay out cooked bacon on a baking sheet, each piece overlapping the next. The idea is to make a square bacon sheet to serve as the wrap for the fast food sushi.

A2. Make sure to place your sushi roller under the bacon mat. This will help in the actual rolling of the sushi.

A3. Take all the buns off the burgers and cut them into thirds. Lay out the fries horizontally onto the bacon. Make sure you don't put too many French fries down: the length should be the same as that of the bacon mat; the width should be 3 to 5 French fries. Once it's all on the bacon mat, use your sushi roller and ROLL ONE UP, HOMIE!

NUGGET NIGIRI

B1. The chicken nugget nigiri is simple. Use 3 to 5 French fries, 2 strips of uncooked bacon, and 1 chicken nugget. Lay down bacon strips with the fries crosswise in the middle to make a T. Lay the chicken nugget at the center (or where the fries and bacon cross). Fold the bacon strips over so that they hold the fries and nugget in place. Preheat the oven to 350°F. Put chicken nugget nigiris on a baking sheet and leave them in there for 20 minutes, or until the bacon is cooked to your liking.

POPCORN CHICKEN ROLL

C1. Same as A1.

C2. Same as A2.

C3. Lay down fries horizontally onto the bacon sushi roll.

C4. Add popcorn chicken on top of the fries.

C5. Add coleslaw to the top of the chicken.

C6. Roll one up, homie!

SUPREME HANDROLL

D1. Open up the Crunch Wrap Supreme and add the French Fries Supreme. Cut it in half so you're left with two half moons, and then roll it up into a cone. Voilà, supreme hand rolls.

MEATBALL DEATHSTAR

INGREDIENTS

2½ pounds ground beef

½ cup bread crumbs

1 egg white

Salt and pepper

4 bell peppers (green, red, yellow, or orange)

1 large onion

1 pound pancetta (or bacon)

½ garlic bulb

1 small can tomato paste

2 cans tomato puree

2 sticks salted butter

1 bulb garlic

1 large circular loaf bread

1 pound meat-filled pasta

1 wedge Parmesan cheese

1 pound mozzarella

EQUIPMENT

1 round medium-sized casserole dish

1 large pot (for sauce)

+ Maybe one of these,

SERVES: 2 men or 4 little bitches

TOTAL CALORIES
14262

WHAT YOU DON'T KNOW

Sauce Boss used to be a high school teacher before *EpicMealTime*. He taught History class.

DIRECTIONS

MEATBALLS

A1. Mix 2 pounds of ground beef with bread crumbs, egg white, and salt and pepper.

A2. When everything is combined, mold two-thirds of the mixture onto the walls of the casserole dish, creating a hollowed-out semicircle. Throw it in the fridge until you need it.

MEAT SAWCE

B1. Chop up all those vegetables and throw them into the pot on high heat (wait until step 3 before adding garlic).

B2. Chop pancetta into little squares.

B3. Once the onions have become soft and see-through, add the pancetta and garlic to the mix.

B4. When the fancy bacon and vegetables are soft, mix in the tomato paste.

B5. Follow that up by adding the remaining ½ pound of ground beef. Cook until meat is light brown.

B6. Add tomato puree and stir.

B7. Let sit on low heat until you are ready to use.

GARLIC BUTTER BATH

C1. Melt all that butter in a small pot. Let sit on low heat.

C2. Chop up some garlic and add it to the butter.

C3. Leave on low heat until the garlic has turned see-through.

C4. Let sit until it's ready to be added to the bread.

C5. Slice the bread in half. Apply the garlic butter to the bread.

C6. Put bread in the oven on broil until it turns crispy.

DEATHSTAR FILLING (STUFFED PASTA)

D1. Boil some water in a pot and add the stuffed pasta of your choice.

D2. When pasta is done, use half the meat sawce and mix the pasta and sauce together.

DEATHSTAR

E1. Preheat the oven to 395°F. Put as much pasta and meat sauce in the the meat mold as it can hold.

E2. Grate half the cheese on the top of the pasta before closing the DeathStar up.

E3. Use the remaining ground meat for the cover of the DeathStar.

E4. Press the ground-meat top with the base of the DeathStar so that they cook and cure together in the oven.

E5. Cover the DeathStar with tinfoil and put into the oven for 45 minutes to 1 hour (if the ball isn't cooked after 1 hour, let it go until it's done or the meat reaches 170°F).

BUILD THE DEATHSTAR MEATBALL

F1. Flip the casserole dish so that the meatball slides out onto the large circular garlic bread (the bread and ball should be on a cookie sheet so you can put it in the oven once more).

F2. Smother that bitch in Meat Sawce and mozzarella.

F3. Put it in the oven on broil (500°F) for 10 minutes (or until the cheese on top is bubbling).

F4. Take out of the oven and get your dumbest friend to eat it.

Step B2

Step D1

Step E2

Step F2

SLAUGHTERHOUSE (X-MAS SPECIAL)

INGREDIENTS

5 pounds bacon

1 carton eggnog

1 large bottle whiskey

+ cinnamon

+ brown sugar

2 large uncut beef tenderloins

3 sticks butter

3 pounds baby back ribs

½ liter Coca-Cola

1½ pounds ground pork

10 pork sausage links (preferably honey garlic)

2 packs puff pastry

5 Yukon Gold potatoes

5 sweet potatoes

2 jars Cheez Whiz

1 package sliced deli ham

EQUIPMENT

1 large saucepan

1 medium saucepan

1 cookie sheet

1 deep-dish roasting pan

1 metal strainer

1 mixing bowl

1 mason jar

4 metal grills (for supporting the walls)

+ cooking twine

+ long skewers

SERVES:

2 men or 4 little bitches

TOTAL CALORIES

8 6 9 9 7

IF YOU DON'T KNOW, NOW YOU KNOW

Shout-outs go to Heather, Gillian, Lindsay, Heather, Norma, and Gail.

DIRECTIONS

WHISKEY BACON GREASE EGGNOG

A1. Chop 1 pound of bacon into bits and cook on high heat.

A2. Extract the bacon grease using metal strainer.

A3. Add 1 part bacon grease to 3 parts eggnog and 1 part whiskey.

CANDY BACON

B1. Lay the reamaining bacon strips on a cookie sheet lined with tinfoil.

B2. Mix equal parts cinnamon and brown sugar.

B3. Coat the bacon strips with the sugar mixture and bake at 375°F for 10 minutes.

B4. Flip the strips and reapply the sugar mixture.

B5. Bake for another 10 minutes.

B6. Remove when bubbling and set aside to harden.

BEEF TENDERLOIN BRICKS

C1. Preheat the oven to 450°F.

C2. Cut the loins into 1-inch-thick pieces.

C3. In a large sauté pan, add 1 stick of butter and sear each side of the loin.

C4. Place each seared piece of loin into a deep-dish roasting pan.

C5. Throw the roasting pan into the oven until the internal temperature of the meat is 115 to 120°F.

C6. Each loin should yield about 20 bricks for the slaughterhouse walls (10 bricks each side).

WHISKEY COKE RIBS

D1. Preheat the oven to 325°F.

D2. Fill a large saucepan to the brim with baby back ribs and steam using Coke.

D3. After about 20 minutes, throw ribs into a large roasting pan and cover with whiskey and more Coke.

D4. Bake for 20 to 25 minutes (or until darkened).

HONEY GARLIC GROUND PORK MEAT GLUE

E1. Combine equal parts ground pork and honey garlic sausage in mixing bowl.

E2. The more you mix, the stronger the meat glue.

E3. Set aside for construction.

GROUND PORK MEAT FOUNDATION

F1. Preheat the oven to 350°F.

F2. Cover a cookie sheet with 1 pound of ground pork (creating a meat base).

F3. Bake until meat has turned a light golden-brown color (15 to 20 minutes).

Step C2

Step C3

Step D3

Step F2

WHAT YOU ONLY WISH YOU KNEW

Adam Pooyay, a dedicated fan, tattooed the *EpicMealTime* logo across his entire back.

DIRECTIONS

PUFF PASTRY ROOF

G1. How many puff pastry shingles you use depends on how large your meat construction is.

G2. Lay out the pastries on a cookie sheet and bake (follow the instructions on the box).

MASHED POTATO GARDENS

H1. Peel and boil Yukon Gold potatoes.

H2. You'll know they're done when you stick a fork in one and the potatoes don't stick to the fork.

H3. Dump potatoes in a large saucepan and add one stick of butter. Mash 'em up!

MASHED SWEET POTATO

I1. Repeat above using sweet potatoes.

CHEEZ WHIZ

J1. In a large saucepan, heat both jars of Cheez Whiz on medium to low heat.

BUILDING

K1. Start by laying the bricks of cooked beef tenderloin in a square shape on top of the ground pork base. Make sure to leave an opening for the door at the very top.

K2. On top of the bricks, spread the mortar or meat glue.

K3. Continue to layer the bricks and mortar until the base of the house is complete.

K4. Using the metal grills for support, apply bricks to the exterior of the base. For extra support, stand up some long skewers on the interior, tying them together with the cooking twine.

K5. Once the bricks and mortar are secure, put them back in the oven at 350°F for about 15 to 20 minutes, or until the meat glue is fully cooked.

K6. In a creative fashion, spread the regular mashed potatoes along the perimeter of the house, simulating snow. This will also act as glue for the rib fence.

K7. Down the middle of the base, extending outward from the door, use the sweet potato mash as a walkway.

K8. Place the ribs with bones facing upward, simulating a fence on the perimeter of the entire tray.

K9. Put the sliced ham on the door opening.

K10. Empty the entire pot of Cheez Whiz into the cavity of the house (The Great Cheese Flood).

K11. Make the roof using a combination of puff pastry and candy bacon. Lay out the pastry on top of the house base and then use the candy bacon as shingles.

K12. Drizzle the bacon bits over the entire creation to simulate a greasy-ass snowstorm.

Step 3

Step 6

Step 10

Step 11

EPIC MOOK

MOOKY GWOPSON

First Episode: Triple Meat Log
Eating Style: Gwopanese
Position: One Half of Team Cuisine

One half of "Team Cuisine," Josh, a.k.a. Epic Mook, is always in the kitchen. He is heavily involved in the planning of meals and the purchasing of new kitchen equipment for episodes. He had no prior kitchen training other than cooking for girls he was trying to put his fingers inside of. Now, with 700+ hours of cooking under his belt through *EpicMealTime*, some would say he is one of the top self-taught online chefs in the world. Others would say he is the only "hater" within *EpicMealTime*. He also helped write this shit book.

IF YOU DON'T KNOW, NOW YOU KNOW

Doctor's warning: *EpicMealTime* is extremely unhealthy and may increase the risk of dirty gut.

"YOU AIN'T SPEAKING THAT GWOPANESE, YOU AIN'T SPEAKING MY LANGUAGE"

BLACK LEGEND

INGREDIENTS

1 box of Chips Ahoy! cookies. (Come to think of it, any packaged chocolate chip cookies will do.)

2 cups of your favorite ixe cream (That's not a spelling mistake, it's motherfuckin' ixe cream.)

1 box easy-make pancake mix (Just add water, ya fuckin' idiot! Don't worry . . . we're dumb too.)

+ Assortment of any 6 cream-filled pastries (I'm the Pablo Escobar of packaged pastries so I don't give a fuck what kind you choose.)

1 liter corn oil

2 cups milk (pregnant milk is my favorite, but I'm a disgusting human being).

1½ cups all-purpose flour

½ cup cocoa powder

½ cup chocolate syrup (sizzurp if you're real G)

6 tablespoons powdered sugar

2 large eggs

2 tablespoons butter, melted

½ teaspoon pure vanilla extract

¼ teaspoon salt

1 Sara Lee Deep 'n Delicious Cake (chocolate)

10 containers white drizz (For drizzing all over your creation at the end . . . it's basically icing, but for drizzing!)

2 chicks, 1 crepe, or make a whole bunch of your dinner guests extra fat by slamming this big 'ol bitch down on the table after a large meal!

SERVES:

TOTAL CALORIES
19177

Our *EpicMealTime* logo is inspired by a collection of shows and video games . . . it's also a pothead!

EQUIPMENT

1 deep fryer or large pot

2 large circular pizza trays

1 large glass bowl

1 small saucepan

10 long skewers

2 mixing bowls (1 medium, 1 large)

+ tinfoil

+ blender or food processor

DIRECTIONS

Preheat the oven to 325°F.

ICE CREAM BALLS

A1. Using your hands,* crush all of the chocolate chip cookies in a medium-size mixing bowl. Show no fuckin' mercy!! Shape as many ice cream balls as you want using your hands. Roll balls around in the crushed cookie mixture, creating an even layer around the frozen balls. Put them in the freezer for at least 20 to 30 minutes to harden (we'll come back to these in a bit).

* Optional: tool for wimps

DEEP-FRIED BATTER AND DEEP-FRYING PASTRIES

B1. In a small mixing bowl, add the suggested amount of water to the easy-make pancake mixture. When using pancake mix for deep-frying, you want to make it a bit thicker by adding more powder than suggested.

B2. For easy dunking, butterfly all your pastries.

B3. Using the long skewers, motherfuckin' slam-dunk the pastries in the deep-fry mixture and then immediately in the 395°F oil until they are a golden brown. Repeat as many times as needed (depending on how many pastries you have).

CHOCOLATE CREPES

C1. Take the remaining ingredients listed and throw them into a mixing apparatus (food processor or blender) until you get a smooth consistency. The more chocolate sawce you add, the darker the crepe. The darker the crepe, the sweeter the dessert.

C2. Add a thin layer of this chocolate mixture onto two pizza trays and bake at 325°F for 120 minutes, or until you see bubbles appear on the surface.

C3. Remove from the oven and let stand. The residual heat will continue to cook the crepes. You know? Motherfuckin' residual heat, son!

ICE CREAM BALLS (CONTINUED)

D1. Once these balls have sat in the freezer, stick a long skewer in them and deep-fry without detaching from the skewer. Only put them in the deep fryer for 10 to 15 seconds so you don't melt the entire ball.

DESSERT GLUE

E1. In a medium mixing bowl, mash up the Deep 'n Delicious Cake creating what we call a chocolate paste. This will be used to fuse the large black crepes together with the deep-fried pastries.

DRIZZED SAWCE

F1. Pour the white drizz into a small saucepan and simmer on low heat until you gain a smooth consistency.

Step A1

Step C2

Step D1

Step E1

Harley writes the voice-over for each episode on his cell phone 2½ minutes prior to recording, the night the video is uploaded.

BUILDING

G1. First move is to combine the two big crepes to form a super large crepe.

G2. Lay out one crepe over another. Use the cake glue to connect the two overlapping sides of the circular crepes.

G3. Lay out the deep-fried pastries in the middle of the double circle, forming a rectangle-like-shape. (Make sure to leave enough space on both sides and ends to close the crepe.)

G4. Using the cake glue, smother the ends so that when you close the crepe, it will stick to the deep-fried pastries.

G5. Take your load of drizz and drizz all over this big ol' beeitch, then top with the deep-fried ice cream balls.

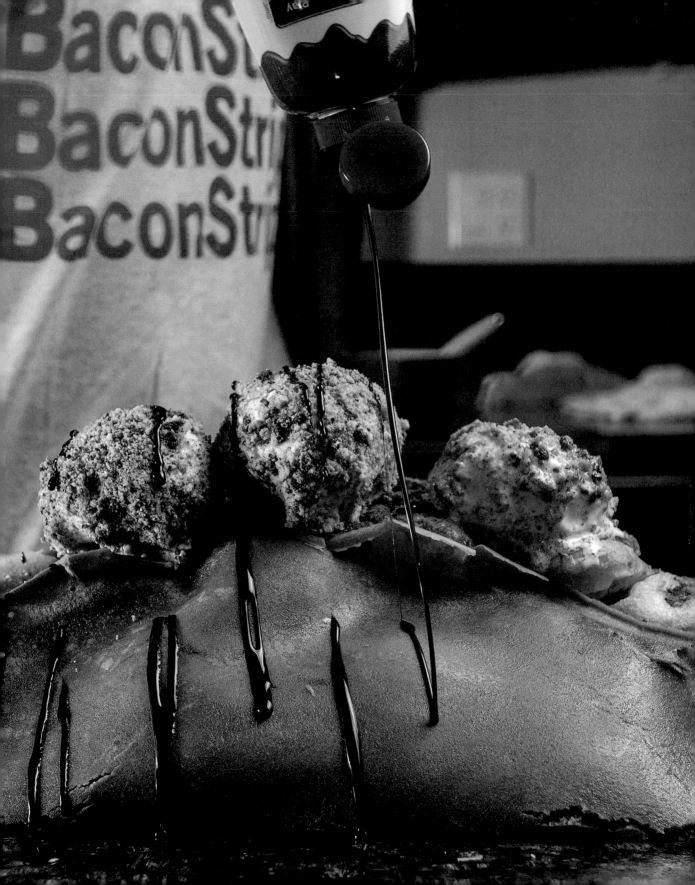

EPIC EGG ROLL

INGREDIENTS

1 liter corn oil

1½ cups all-purpose flour

½ teaspoon salt

2 eggs, beaten

1½ cups cold water

4 tablespoons peanut oil

+ Any 4 meals from your favorite Chinese restaurant

1 egg (beaten to make glue)

I like General Tso's chicken, Cantonese-style chow mein, Hunan dumplings, and chicken fried rice . . . all meals that a stupid white man would like!

EQUIPMENT

1 deep fryer or large pot

1 perforated large deep-frying spoon

YIELDS: *1 big-ass egg roll for somebody's big-ass gut!*

TOTAL CALORIES
6 3 7 8

DIRECTIONS

A1. Heat corn oil in a large pot to about 395°F.

A2. Combine all the dry ingredients in a bowl.

A3. Beat the eggs while adding the water and the peanut oil at the same time.

A4. At this point, you should have 2 bowls: 1 with dry ingredients and 1 with wet ingredients. In a food processor, mix the contents of both bowls together slowly.

A5. Once well blended, remove the batter and knead it with your hands until it forms a dough-like consistency.

BUILDING

B1. Once you've got your Chinese food, it's time to build the thing.

B2. Using the egg-roll dough, create a large circular surface (almost like pizza crust, but thinner).

B3. Dump some of each Chinese dish in the center of the circle. Be careful to leave at least 1 inch of dough around the perimeter.

B4. Using a brush or your hands, slather some beaten egg on one side of the egg-roll dough so that it will stick to the other side when you create the pocket.

B5. Once you've folded it all up, deep-fry it until the egg roll is golden brown.

Now what the fuck is up?! Let all those motherfuckers know that you don't fuck around when it comes to egg rolls!!

Step B2

Step B3

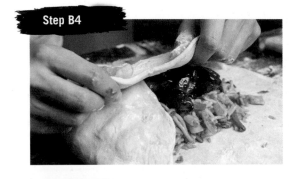

Step B4

Step B5

CHILI 4 LOKO

INGREDIENTS

7 pounds bacon

1 large onion

2 pounds ground pork

1 liter (32 ounces) corn oil

5 Italian sausages, or pepperoni

1 pound Canadian back bacon

1 medium-sized deli ham

2 28-ounce cans tomato sawce

1 small can tomato paste

3–5 jalapeño peppers

1 28-ounce can assorted bean mix

1 30-ounce package French fries

2 eggs

1 big bag Miss Vickie's jalapeño potato chips

10 cheese sticks

1 large bag shredded cheddar cheese

1 16-ounce container sour cream

1 can Four Loko (optional)

4 crazy sons of bitches. This chili actually makes you go crazy. Muscles Glasses has not been the same ever since he ate it. He's a little fatter now, too.

SERVES:

♟♟♟♟♟

TOTAL CALORIES

46255

IF YOU DON'T KNOW, NOW YOU KNOW

Cousin Dave has five level-85 characters in World of Warcraft.

EQUIPMENT

1 large trough-style casserole dish

2 large pots (for deep frying and making chili)

1 medium saucepan

2 small containers

DIRECTIONS
BACON TROUGH

A1. Preheat the oven to 395°F.

A2. Use as many bacon strips as needed to line the inside of the trough-style casserole dish.

A3. The dish will probably need at least 2 grease drains.

A4. Once the bacon is cooked, take it out and set aside.

Put the corn oil into a large pot and heat to 375°F.

Increase the heat of the oven to 450°F for the fries.

CHILI

B1. Dice 4 pounds of bacon into bits. Cook them up in a medium saucepan until they are dark and crispy. Set aside until needed for chili.

B2. Dice up the onion and sauté until the onions are translucent.

B3. At the same time the onions are frying up, brown the ground pork in the large pot. Once the ground meat is brown and the onions are translucent, add the bacon bits and the onions to the ground pork mixture.

B4. Empty out the sausages into the chili mixture and continue cooking on medium to high heat.

B5. Dice the Canadian back bacon and the ham and add to the pot. Add the pepperoni or Italian sausages.

B6. At the point where the meat is cooking, add the tomato sawce and the tomato paste.

B7. Let this cook down for about 15 to 20 minutes.

B8. After it has cooked down, dice up the jalapeños and add to the mixture. Then add the bean mixture and let cook down again for 15 to 25 minutes.

FRENCH FRIES

C1. Usually frozen French fries take about 15 to 20 minutes at 450°F depending on the brand. Follow the directions.

C2. When the fries are done, set aside until it's time to build.

Step B1

Step B3

Step B8

Step C2

Step D4

Step E1

Step E4

Step E5

MISS VICKIE'S CHEESE STICKS

D1. Crack and beat two eggs in a small bowl.

D2. Empty out the chips into another bowl and crush them up. This will be used for deep-frying.

D3. Dunk the cheese sticks in the eggs and then immediately in the crushed-up chips. This will create a potato chip crust for the cheese sticks.

D4. Carefully dunk in the hot oil for about 15 seconds, making sure that the cheese doesn't melt.

D5. Repeat process with all of the cheese sticks you have.

BUILDING

E1. Using the French fries, create a layer on the base of the bacon trough.

E2. Take a handful of cheddar cheese and create a second layer on top of the fries.

E3. Cover up the whole base with as much chili as you can.

E4. Using the deep-fried cheese sticks, create a top layer over the chili; then, using a handful of cheddar cheese, make another layer on top of the chili.

E5. Put the whole trough in the oven on broil, until the cheese has melted and becomes golden brown.

E6. When the top is done, take out of the oven and slap a whole bunch of sour cream onto the top.

*Four Loko addition

If you are feeling epic, punch some holes into the base of the chili trough and add some Loko.

PRINCE ATARI

AMEER ATARI

First Episode: Angry French Canadian
Eating Style: Great White Shark Attack
Position: One Half of Team Cuisine

Ameer moved from the ghettos of Montreal to the video game kiosks of Oklahoma and then back to Montreal. He has been a huge help in the kitchen. The other half of "Team Cuisine," Ameer was raised creating munchies for himself with whatever he could find lying around. This made him very resourceful. Think large steak-and-gravy burritos and nacho rangoon all sprinkled with meth. Ameer is what we refer to as a "Unique." A Unique is a type of person who most of you will never know/meet. They are people who are so strange, they don't even know themselves. They wake up every day a new person, not knowing what they felt the day before or what they will feel the next day. This type of person latches himself onto consistencies such as "bacon tastes good" and "liquor gets you drunk." This makes our Unique extremely passionate about eating bacon and getting drunk no matter "who" he is that day.

IF YOU DON'T KNOW, NOW YOU KNOW

The first three episodes of *EpicMealTime* are based on still-unpublished portions of the Dead Sea Scrolls. This will all make sense on June 13, 2009.

"YOU PUT IT IN THE OVEN, AND THEN YOU WIN"

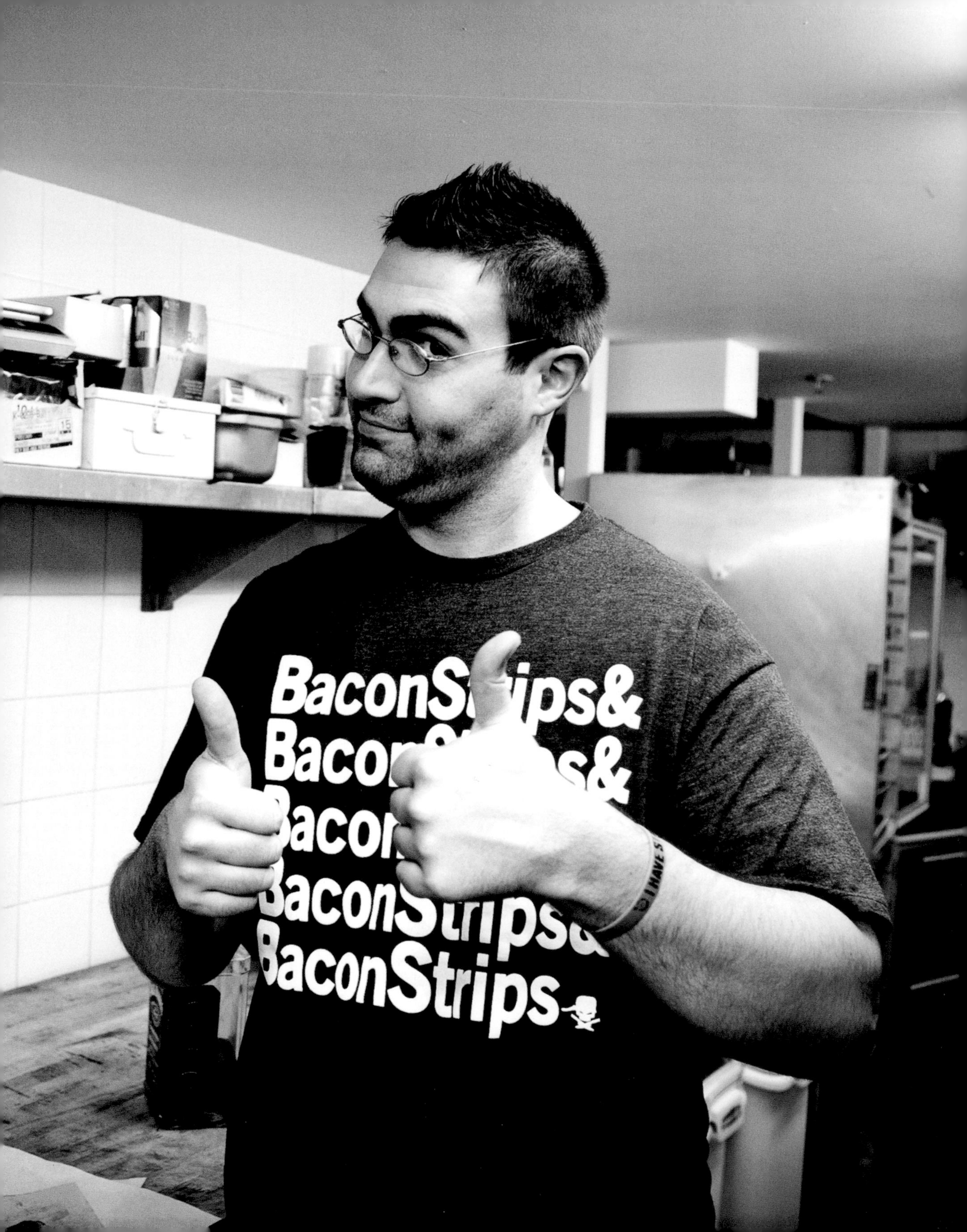
BaconStrips&
BaconStrips

MEAT SALAD

INGREDIENTS

+ Soy sawce
+ Worcestershire sawce
+ Salt and pepper

3 large, uncut flank steaks

1 liter corn oil

6 eggs

2 cups all-purpose flour

1 16-ounce container bread crumbs

2 cans beer

4 boneless, skinless chicken breasts

2 pounds ground beef

+ Ketchup
+ BBQ sawce

4 pounds bacon

6 pork sausages

10 pepperoni sticks

1 ready-to-eat holiday ham

1 large salami

EQUIPMENT

1 frying pan

1 medium saucepan

1 Ziploc bag

3 medium containers

1 large salad bowl

1 deep-dish sauté pan

SERVES: *2 men or 4 little bitches*

TOTAL CALORIES

2 8 0 3 1

DIRECTIONS

FLANK STEAK LETTUCE

A1. Preheat the oven to 395°F.

A2. Pour soy sawce, Worcestershire sawce, and salt and pepper to taste into a Ziploc bag. Add steaks and marinate. The longer you marinate them, the better they will taste.

A3. Remove the steaks from the marinade. Discard the marinade. On medium to high heat, sear the steaks until they have a thin crust.

A4. Put the crusted steaks in the oven for about 30 to 35 minutes. Remove and let stand for at least 10 minutes.

FRIED CHICKEN LETTUCE

B1. In the deep-dish frying pan, heat 1 inch of cooking oil to 395°F.

B2. Using three medium containers, prepare dredging stations: 4 eggs in the first container, flour in the second, and 2 cups of breadcrumbs in the third. Add beer to the egg mixture if you're feeling gangster!

B3. Using a huge mallet or anything else to smack raw chicken with, beat the meat until it is ¼ inch thick.

B4. Now dunk that meat in flour, then egg, and then breadcrumbs.

B5. Once your oil is hot, fry the battered-up chicken until golden brown on both sides.

B6. Put the chicken aside to settle.

MEATBALL RADISHES

C1. In a large mixing bowl place the ground beef, an egg or two (depending on how much ground beef you use), ½ cup of breadcrumbs, ketchup or BBQ sawce, and salt and pepper to taste. Mix until the whole concoction is one consistency.

C2. Using your hands, roll the meat into golf ball–sized meatballs and put them in the fridge for 15 minutes to allow the meat to settle.

C3. In a frying pan on medium heat, fry up the meatballs until they are brown on the outside and firm in texture.

BACON BITS / BACON GARNISH

D1. Preheat the oven to 380°F.

D2. Chop 3 pounds of bacon into small pieces.

D3. In a medium saucepan, cook the bacon bits on high heat until they are brown and crispy. Add beer to the bacon bit mixture if you're still feeling gangster!

D4. You will use these as a garnish for the salad.

D5. Bake the remaining bacon for 20 minutes, flipping and degreasing at the 10-minute mark. This will be used as a bacon border garnish.

SAUSAGE CUCUMBERS

E1. Using a frying pan, cook the sausages until they reach a texture you are comfortable with. Slice them on a diagonal to simulate cucumbers.

PEPPERONI CARROT STICKS

F1. Slice the pepperoni sticks into long matchsticks to simulate carrots. No cooking is necessary.

HAM CROUTONS

G1. Slice up a ready-to-eat holiday ham into 1-inch thick slices.

G2. Cut the border off each slice and then dice up into crouton-shaped ham pieces.

SALAMI TOMATOES

H1. Cut whole salami in half, lengthwise.

H2. Chop into 1-inch thick pieces. The idea is to make half-moon-shaped tomato slices. No cooking necessary.

BUILDING

I1. Just like you would build any meat salad, throw it into a giant bowl and toss!

I2. Add the bacon bits and bacon border and the beer bacon salad dressing, and then have your carnivore friends eat it.

Step I1

Step I2

SLOPPY ROETHLISBURGER

INGREDIENTS

4 tablespoons active dry yeast

2 cups plus 2 tablespoons warm water (110° to 115°)

½ cup vegetable oil

½ cup sugar

2 eggs

2 teaspoons salt

6–6½ cups all-purpose flour

2 cups poppy seeds

3 cups chopped onion

8 cloves garlic, finely chopped

8 cups Jack Daniels

4 cups ketchup

1 cup vinegar

6 tablespoons Worcestershire sauce

1 cup brown sugar, firmly packed

1½ cups molasses

1 teaspoon pepper

1 tablespoon salt

½ cup tomato paste

1 teaspoon Liquid Smoke

½ teaspoon Tabasco sauce, or to taste

20 pounds bacon

13 pounds ground beef

11 pounds sausage

12 eggs

5 cups bread crumbs

2 pounds Velveeta cheese or 2 jars Cheez Whiz

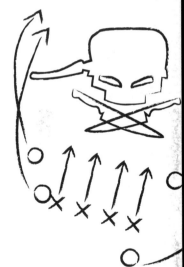

SERVES: 10

TOTAL CALORIES

1 3 8 2 2 6

EQUIPMENT

2 large mixing bowls

2 medium saucepans

1 large stockpot

Food processor

Steaming apparatus

3 large deep-dish circular roasting pans

Meat thermometer

1 extra-large cookie sheet for the hamburger bun

Giant tube to blow the BBQ sauce

DIRECTIONS

GIANT HAMBURGER BUN

A1. In a large bowl, dissolve yeast in warm water. Add oil and sugar; let stand for 5 minutes. Add the eggs, salt, and enough flour to form a soft dough.

A2. Turn onto a floured surface; knead until smooth and elastic, about 3 to 5 minutes. Do not let rise.

A3. Cover and let rest for 10 minutes. Preheat the oven to 425°F.

A4. Form the dough into a large ball and put onto the cookie sheet.

A5. Let bake for 25 to 35 minutes or until golden brown.

A6. For extra *EMT* effects, print out and then cut out an *EMT* logo. When the bun is hot and out of the oven, use the cutout to make your logo on the bun using the poppy seeds.

JACK DANIELS BBQ SAUCE

B1. Cook the onions and garlic until translucent, about 10 to 20 minutes.

B2. Combine onions, garlic, and Jack Daniels in a stockpot.

B3. Add all remaining ingredients and then bring to boil.

B4. Simmer uncovered until reduced and thickened, about 15 to 25 minutes.

B5. Add more Jack Daniels if a stronger flavor is desired.

BACON SAUSAGE BEEF ROETHLISBURGER

C1. Preheat the oven to 400°F.

C2. Chop up 10 pounds of the bacon into ¾-inch pieces.

Step A6

Step B5

WHAT YOU ONLY WISH YOU KNEW

Originally, Bill Murray was to be cast as the host of *EpicMealTime* but we don't have his contact information. If any of you know Bill Murray, tell him we want him on the show.

C3. Put the chopped bacon into the steaming apparatus and let steam until the bacon is fully cooked through.

C4. Add the steamed bacon to the food processor and blend until it becomes the consistency of ground meat.

C5. In a large mixing bowl, combine the ground beef, ground bacon, and the insides of the sausages to create one consistency. Add eggs and bread crumbs to the mixture.

C6. Fill the three large circular roasting pans with the meat concoction.

C7. Put in oven until the inside of the meat is at least 160°F and there are no visible pink areas.

BACON STRIPS

D1. Preheat the oven to 380°F.

D2. Line cookie sheet with the remaining bacon strips.

D3. Flip and degrease every 10 minutes until the strips have become the consistency you like.

Step D3

CHEESE SAWCE

E1. In a medium saucepan, follow the instructions to melt Velveeta cheese. Usually this means putting it on medium heat and adding cream or milk.

Step C5

Step E1

BUILDING

F1. Split the bun and place the bottom half on a flat surface.

F2. Each extra-large burger should be cut so that it looks like 1 giant patty.

F3. Once that is done, put the giant 3-piece patty on the bottom layer of the bun.

F4. Take your melted cheese and slather the entire top of the meat patty.

F5. Apply as many bacon strips as your heart desires.

F6. Using a giant tube, BLOW the BBQ sawce on the top of the cheese.

F7. Complete this sloppy burger by putting on the top half of the bun.

Step F1

Step F2

Step F4

Step F5

TEQUILA TACO NIGHT

INGREDIENTS

10 pounds bacon

12 cups all-purpose flour

1 teaspoon baking powder

3 teaspoons salt

1 stick salted butter

½ cup heavy cream

2 cups shortening or lard

3 cups warm water

2 thin-cut steaks

4 boneless, skinless chicken breasts

1 bottle tequila

½ cup BBQ sauce

5 jalapeño peppers

1 pound ground beef

1 16-ounce jar roasted red peppers

6 avocados

6 ripe tomatoes

3 large red onions

+ juice of 2 limes

3 cloves garlic

1 16-ounce package Mexican rice

1 pound Velveeta cheese, cubed

+ cream or milk

2 bags Mexican-style shredded cheese

2 cups sour cream

2 33-ounce cans refried beans

1 bushel cilantro

YIELDS: *Enough to get 3 people full and drunk!*

TOTAL CALORIES
98824

WHAT YOUR MOM KNOWS

Every member of *EpicMealTime* likes to wear jeans when they get into a hot tub.

EQUIPMENT

1 large circular roasting pan (shallow)

1 frying pan

2 Ziploc bags

2 large mixing bowls

1 food processor

1 rolling pin

2 cookie sheets

+ tinfoil

DIRECTIONS

BACON BURRITO/QUESADILLA DOUGH

A1. Chop 5 pounds bacon into bits and cook in a medium saucepan until crispy.

A2. Drain the grease and set aside for dough.

A3. In a large bowl combine the flour, baking powder, and salt.

A4. Add 1 stick of butter and ½ cup of heavy cream. (If you want maximum flavor, add some of the extracted bacon grease.)

A5. Add shortening and mix until it's the consistency of coarse cornmeal. Add warm (not hot!) water and mix thoroughly. Your dough should be very soft. (Note: It is important that the water be warm, never hot, as this will further precook your tortilla dough and your tortilla will not be as flexible as desired.)

A6. Knead the bacon bits into the dough until combined.

A7. Set dough aside until ready to build.

TEQUILA STEAK / CHICKEN / BACON / GROUND BEEF

B1. Slice up steaks and chicken and put into separate Ziploc bags.

B2. Mix in tequila and BBQ sauce and let marinate for as long as you want. (The longer you let the meat marinate, the better tasting it will be.)

B3. In a large frying pan, cook each type of meat separately.

B4. When cooking the tequila bacon be sure to add some sliced jalapeños.

B5. Once the rest of the meat is cooked, add the ground beef and some roasted red peppers for flavor. Make sure to save some peppers for the cheese sauce.

TEQUILA GUACAMOLE

C1. Slice the avocados in half and remove the pits. Make sure to keep the pits as you'll need them later.

C2. Scoop out the avocado flesh into a large bowl.

C3. Chop up 3 tomatoes and 1½ red onions and add them to the bowl.

C4. Add 3 tablespoons of lime juice to the bowl.

C5. Chop up the garlic and add it as well.

C6. Mix all of the ingredients together then add some tequila. (Feel free to use as much as you want!)

C7. In order to keep the guacamole fresh, place the avocado pits back into the mixture. For some strange reason, this keeps the guac from oxidizing and changing color.

Step B2

Step B5

Step C3

Step C6

FAT COUNTER
175 g of fat
2312 calories

WHAT YOU DON'T KNOW

Muscles Glasses has a detachable penis that is also a combat knife.

DIRECTIONS

BACON STRIPS NACHO CHIPS

D1. Preheat the oven to 395°F. This high temperature will ensure the strips get extra crispy.

D2. On a baking sheet, lay out 2 pounds of bacon strips to be used as nacho chips.

D3. Flip and degrease at least twice.

BACON-WEAVE TACO SHELL

E1. Using the remaining bacon, make sure to start this process on a baking sheet.

E2. It is important to weave together each and every piece of bacon. In order to do this you must lay out the strips vertically with each bacon strip touching the next.

E3. Flip up every second strip enough so that you can put a horizontal strip along the bacon that is not flipped up.

E4. Put the already flipped strips down on the horizontal strip and then flip up the opposite strips. Lay another horizontal strip along the bacon that is lying down.

E5. Repeat the process until you have a bacon weave.

Step E5

MEXICAN RICE

F1. Follow the instructions on the package. Add water and cook while stirring for about 5 minutes.

F2. Set rice aside until ready to build.

CUSTOM CHEESE SAWCE

G1. Cut the Velveeta cheese into cubes and put in a large pot. Add some cream or milk.

G2. Once the cheese is melted, add roasted red peppers for Mexican flavor.

BUILDING

EL GIGANTE BURRITO

H1. Preheat the oven to 350°F.

H2. Flatten the bacon burrito dough into the shape of a circle.(The larger the circle, the larger the burrito.)

H3. In the middle (leaving space around the outside) stack up the steak, chicken, bacon, guac, salsa, shredded cheese, sour cream, and refried beans. Add rice.

H4. To close the burrito, start by flipping one side over horizontally. Then, take one end and flip it inward. You should be left with one long side and one end not turned in.

H5. At this point, repeat the process for the opposite sides to close the burrito.

H6. Put "El Gigante" in the oven for at least 30 minutes or until the dough is cooked completely.

Step G1

Step G2

Step H2

Step H4

Step I3

Step I6

Step J3

Step K1

QUESADILLA

I1. Preheat the oven to 350°F.

I2. Spray a large circular tray with PAM or any other lubricating cooking spray.

I3. Knead the dough so it covers the large circular tray completely.

I4. Bake for 30 minutes.

I5. Remove and let cool.

I6. Cut the shell in half and build your quesadilla using the same ingredients as the burrito.

I7. Close the quesadilla by placing one half on top of the other.

BACON STRIPS NACHO CHIPS

J1. Grab that same circular cookie sheet.

J2. Dress these bacon nachos as you would any tortilla chips.

J3. Layer with cheese, refried beans, tequila guacamole, and salsa. Top it all off with sour cream.

BACON TACOS

K1. On one side of the bacon-weave taco shell lay out the sour cream, ground beef, tequila guacamole, and salsa.

K2. Fold over one side and enjoy.

K3. If you've been taking shots of tequila this whole time, you're hammered now and ready to enjoy your meal!

K4. Bitch.

TEQUILA SALSA

L1. Chop 1½ red onions.

L2. Chop 3 ripe tomatoes.

L3. Chop a bushel of cilantro.

L4. Place in a mixing bowl.

L5. Add ½ cup tequila to the mix.

COUSIN DAVE

DAVID HEUFF

First Episode: Triple Meat Log
Eating Style: Fancy
Position: Fancy Bastard

David is somehow related to every person on the planet; nobody is ever a stranger to him. He's humble, kind, and intelligent. A steady hand has earned David the opportunity to be the cameraman on *EpicMealTime*. Did I mention he practically fuckin' eats cigarettes?! If you've ever seen bacon grease dripping or anyone drinking, there's a good chance that Cousin Dave filmed it. The only one on *EpicMealTime* who actually uses cutlery, David has been given the nickname "Fancy Bastard" among the other team members. In a way, the fact that he uses cutlery on a show where people use their hands to eat has made him the kind of guy who doesn't give a shit about a crew of dudes who don't give a shit. "NotGivingAFuckCeption"?!

IF YOU DON'T KNOW, NOW YOU KNOW

Before Fancy Bastard made *EpicMealTime*, he was working on an online children's show.

"WOW THAT'S GOOD"

MEAT CAR

INGREDIENTS

- **1** pound bacon strips
- **3** large potatoes
- **1** stick butter
- **½** cup heavy cream
- **1** box macaroni and cheese
- **1** cup bread crumbs
- **1** egg
- **+** ketchup
- **1** pound ground beef
- **1** liter cooking oil
- **5** boxes instant pancake mix
- **1** can beer
- **1** salami
- **1** large white onion
- **+** black candy spray paint
- **+** chrome candy sparkles

EQUIPMENT

- **1** cookie sheet
- **+** tinfoil
- **1** large pot
- **1** potato masher ('cause you ain't got Muscles Glasses)
- **1** large mixing bowl
- **+** plastic wrap
- **1** deep-frying lowering apparatus (it may help to use your ingenuity and make one)
- **+** long wooden skewers

YIELDS: *Enough to make it on late-night television!*

SAWCE

TOTAL CALORIES
2 3 2 6 6

WHAT YOUR MOM KNOWS

EpicMealTime filmed a pilot for a TV show in 2011.

DIRECTIONS

BACON STRIPS

A1. Cover a cookie sheet with tinfoil and then lay out the bacon strips on top.

A2. Bake at 395°F for 15 minutes. Drain the bacon grease and flip the strips. Cook for another 15 minutes.

A3. Save some of the bacon grease for the mashed potatoes.

MASHED POTATOES

B1. Peel potatoes and place in a large pot filled with water.

B2. Boil the potatoes. (You will know they are done when you can easily stick a fork into them without it sticking.)

B4. Add butter and heavy cream. (For maximum flavor, add some of the extracted bacon grease, too.)

B5. Using the potato masher, mash the potatoes until they are a smooth and creamy texture.

MAC 'N CHEESE

C1. Make a box of macaroni and cheese any way you like it.

C2. Set aside until it's time to construct.

MEAT CAR BASE

D1. Preheat the oven to 395°F.

D2. In a large mixing bowl, combine bread crumbs, egg, and 3 tablespoons of ketchup. Stir until you reach a consistent texture.

D3. Use the plastic wrap as a base for the meat blanket. Spread the meat over the wrap, leaving a 1-inch border on each side. The blanket should be about ¼-inch thick. The idea is to be able to wrap the potatoes, bacon, and mac 'n cheese in the blanket.

D4. Start laying out the bacon strips 1 inch from the top of the blanket. Add the mashed potatoes on top of the bacon strip layer. Following the same pattern, add the next layer of the mac 'n cheese.

D5. Use the plastic wrap to start the rolling process. Begin with the side where you left 1 inch of uncovered meat. Start rolling the meat (always holding onto the plastic wrap). Twist the plastic wrap on each end of the log as tight as you can. This will help tighten the log as well. Put the log in the fridge for 10 minutes.

D6. When the log is cold, remove the plastic wrap. Be careful that the base doesn't fall apart. Now, wrap the log in tinfoil.

D7. Bake for 30 to 45 minutes.

Step D3

Step D4

Step D4

Step D6

EpicMealTime had already cooked 750 pounds of bacon by their 50th episode.

DEEP-FRYING

E1. Preheat cooking oil to 400°F. (Use a thermometer to confirm temperature.)

E2. In a large mixing bowl, prepare pancake mix with beer instead of water or milk.

E3. After the meat base has cooled, smother the entire thing with pancake batter.

E4. Using your deep-frying lowering apparatus, lower the meat structure into the hot oil until the batter is golden brown. (Use caution . . because it's HOT!)

E5. Take out the deep-fried meat base and set aside.

ONION SALAMI WHEELS

F1. Slice the salami in 1-inch circles to simulate wheels.

F2. Cut the onion in circles so that they'll fit around the salami slices.

F3. Carefully slip the onion rings around the salami wheels so they stay in place.

F4. Smother each wheel with the remaining pancake mix.

F5. Using long wooden skewers to hold the wheels, dip each one into the hot oil until the crust is golden brown.

F6. Remove and set aside for building.

BUILDING

WHEELS

G1. Cut a hole in a piece of paper that's a little smaller than the diameter of the onion salami wheels. Use this as a guide to spray-paint (using candy paint) what looks like a rubber wheel onto the deep-fried salami. While the paint is still wet, apply the chrome candy sparkles to simulate mag wheels.

G2. Repeat for each wheel.

CONNECTING THE WHEELS TO THE BASE

H1. Pierce the long wooden skewers through the meat base on each end of the car, where the wheels would typically go.

H2. Poke each wheel onto the end of a skewer in order to keep wheels in place.

PAINTING THE CAR

I1. Find a picture of flames online. Print it and cut the flames out, so you can use them as a pattern.

I2. Paint the flames on each side of the car using ketchup as paint.

I3. If you can't find a good picture of flames, or are not artistically able to do this step, use your black candy paint to draw racing stripes down the middle of the base.

I4. Now get drunk and race your damn car with your friends before you eat it!

Step E3

Step E5

Step F3

Step F4

FAST FOOD LASAGNA

INGREDIENTS

5 pounds bacon

1 large onion

1 pound ground beef

6 Italian sausages

1 large can tomato sauce

1 bottle whiskey

15 Teen Burgers (A&W), vegetables removed

15 Big Macs (McDonald's)

15 Baconators (Wendy's)

3 large packs shredded mozzarella cheese

1 liter Big Mac Sauce (McDonald's)

7 orders onion rings (A&W)

SERVES: 15

TOTAL CALORIES

7 1 4 8 8

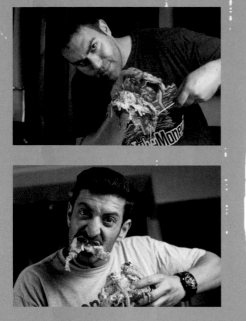

When we decided to make this episode, we had no idea it was going to be our most popular one.

EQUIPMENT

1 large soup pot

1 large baking tray

1 large buffet style-serving try (heat resistant) or 1 large rectangular roasting pan—large enough to fit 3 layers of 15 burgers each

DIRECTIONS
WHISKEY MEAT SAUCE

A1. Chop 1 pound of bacon into bits and put in a large soup pot. Cook bacon until fully browned and crispy (extract bacon grease).

A2. Chop up the onion and add to bacon bits. Fry in large pot until onions are translucent.

A3. Using the same pot, add ground beef and sausage meat and cook through until browned.

A4. Add the large can of tomato sauce and as much whiskey as you desire.

A5. Cook sauce for at least 30 minutes.

BACON STRIP LAYERS

B1. Preheat the oven to 380°F.

B2. Using the baking tray, place each strip of bacon, layering each slightly over the other. The idea is to create a large bacon strip to separate each layer of burger.

B3. Flip and degrease every 10 minutes until the strips have become the consistency you like (crispy is better). Repeat until you have three layers of bacon strips.

BUILDING

Between each layer, take a flat surface and flatten down the burgers. This will help contain all three layers and 45 burgers.

C1. Preheat the oven to 385°F.

C2. Add 1 layer of 15 burgers to the roasting pan.

C3. Fill the next layer with bacon strips.

C4. On top of the bacon strips layer, add a thick layer of liquor meat sauce followed by another layer of shredded mozzarella cheese.

C5. Lay down another 15 burgers on top of the cheese layer followed by another bacon layer on top of the second layer of burgers.

C6. Use a spoon or spatula to spread Big Mac Sauce over the bacon strips layer, followed by another layer of shredded mozzarella cheese.

C7. Lay the last of the 15 burgers and press the entire lasagna down as much as you can without compromising the look of the dish.

C8. Add the remains of the meat sauce as the next layer.

C9. Seal in all that flavor with the last layer of bacon strips.

C10. The second-to-last layer should be onion rings, followed by a thin layer of shredded cheese.

C11. Put the entire lasagna in the oven for 15 minutes.

Step C2

Step C3

Step C4

CANDY BBQ

INGREDIENTS

1 liter cooking oil

1 16-ounce bag milk chocolate chips

1 box rice crispies

1 roll cookie dough

1 box instant pancake batter

4 containers cotton candy (16 ounces total)

5 packs Kit Kat bars

1 cup all-purpose flour

2 16-ounce jars Marshmallow Fluff

1 16-ounce bag peanut M&M's

Assorted donuts (at least 4 strudel-style Danishes)

Random assorted jelly candies that look like lettuce/tomatoes/pickles

1 32-ounce pack gay bacon strips

Red icing

Yellow icing

Green icing

White icing

4 Oh Henry! bars

1 box fruit roll-ups (preferably yellow)

SERVES: *6 of your friends but no diabetics.*

TOTAL CALORIES

49885

IF YOU DON'T KNOW, NOW YOU KNOW

This recipe was the birth of gay bacon strips.

EQUIPMENT

1 large soup pot

1 large mixing bowl

1 deep-dish baking tray

1 oversized circular cookie cutter

+ Tinfoil T-bone steak–shaped mold

1 perforated heat-resistant spoon

1 large glass bowl

1 Cutting board

1 glass bowl

1 Candy thermometer

DIRECTIONS
DEEP-FRYING OIL

A1. In a large soup pot, heat cooking oil to 395°F and set aside for Kit-Kat French fries.

CHOCOLATE SAWCE

B1. Pour chocolate chips into a glass bowl and microwave for 3 to 4 minutes on high. Take it out and stir well halfway through.

B2. Put bowl back in the microwave for 2 more minutes on high, take it out and stir well once again. At this point in time, you will notice that about ¼ of the chocolate has started to melt.

B3. Microwave for 30 seconds more on high—take it out and stir well. Now you will see that about ½ to ⅔ of the chocolate is melted.

B4. Microwave for another 10 seconds, take it out and stir it well once again. You can repeat this process for up to 3 more 10-second intervals.

B5. Once melted, you need to carefully check the temperature of the chocolate using either a digital candy thermometer or a regular one. (You can check the accuracy of your thermometer by putting it in boiling water to see if it can reach 100°F.) This is the crucial point—the chocolate should not be over 89–90°F for dark chocolate, 86°F for milk chocolate, or 84–85°F for white chocolate.

B6. Keep stirring the chocolate for another minute or so, you'll be amazed at how the temperature changes. The chocolate should be glossy and smooth.

Step B6

Step C3

CHOCOLATE RICE CRISPY BURGERS

C1. In a mixing bowl add 2 parts rice crispies to 1 part chocolate sauce.

C2. Work fast at mixing the two together in order to create 1 consistency.

C3. In a deep-dish baking tray spread out the chocolate rice crispies into an even layer.

C4. Put in fridge to cool and harden.

C5. Take the tray out of the fridge and use the cookie cutter to cut out burger shapes.

C6. Set aside until time to build.

COOKIE DOUGH STEAK

D1. Using a tinfoil mold on a cutting board, press out the raw cookie dough (forming a steak).

D2. Drip the remaining chocolate sauce on top and put into fridge to harden.

WHAT YOUR MOM KNOWS

Cotton candy in French is *"barbe a papa."*

DEEP-FRIED BATTER AND KIT KATS

E1. Make instant pancake mix by just adding water.

E2. Pull apart cotton candy and mix into the batter.

E4. In a small bowl, dust the Kit Kats with flour before adding them to the batter.

E5. Batter up the Kit Kats and add no more than 3 to 4 at a time to the hot oil. Adding too many will likely cause them to stick together and not cook properly.

E6. Take Kit Kats out after 8 to 12 seconds or after they have browned.

MARSHMALLOW FLUFF POTATO SALAD

F1. Empty the fluff into a glass bowl.

F2. Empty the bag of M&M's in with fluff and mix.

BUILDING

CANDY BURGERS

G1. Flatten down 2 donuts.

G2. Spread some white icing onto one side of a donut.

G3. Layer the chocolate burger on top of the mayo.

G4. Add some candy jellies.

G5. Add some gay bacon strips.

G6. Finish off with red/yellow/green icing.

* Continue until you have as many burgers as you want.

CANDY HOT DOGS

H1. Slice Danish down the middle.

H2. Add Oh Henry!.

H3. Put candy condiments on top and enjoy.

H4. Repeat with remaining Danishes and candy bars.

Step E5

Step G1

Step G5

Step H3

84-EGG SANDWICH

INGREDIENTS

8 pounds bacon

3 packages active dry yeast

2 cups warm water (110°F)

8 cups bread flour

4 tablespoons olive oil

2 teaspoons salt

4 teaspoons sugar

28 Egg McMuffins

28 Ham McMuffins

12 breakfast sausages

12 eggs

28 Sausage McMuffins

1 bag shredded cheese

SERVES: *10 regular people or 1 Muscles Glasses*

TOTAL CALORIES

48138

Breakfast is everyone on *EMT*'s favorite meal of the day, eaten at any time of the day.

EQUIPMENT

1 large baking sheet

1 large frying pan

1 rolling pin or 1 large cylinder shaped bottle

+ Small bowl / medium bowl / large bowl

+ Small saucepan

DIRECTIONS

BACON STRIPS

A1. Preheat the oven to 380°F.

A2. Line cookie sheets with 6 pounds of bacon strips.

A3. Flip and degrease every 10 minutes until the strips have become the consistency you like.

EGG SANDWICH POCKET PIZZA DOUGH

B1. In a small bowl, dissolve 1½ packages of yeast in 1 cup of warm water. Let stand until creamy, about 10 minutes.

B2. In a large bowl, combine 4 cups bread flour, 2 tablespoons olive oil, 1 teaspoon salt, 2 teaspoons sugar, and the yeast mixture; stir well to combine. Beat well until a stiff dough has formed. Cover and let rise until doubled in volume, about 30 minutes. Meanwhile, preheat the oven to 350°F.

B3. Turn dough out onto a well-floured surface. Form dough into a long rectangle about ½ inch thick.

B4. Place 25 to 30 egg sandwiches of your choice (not the Sausage McMuffins) along half the rectangle.

B5. Using the second half of the rectangle, cover the contents, creating a closed pocket. Use some wash as glue to fasten the pocket.

B6. Place the rectangle on the baking sheet, and bake for 25 minutes.

Repeat this process again for the second half of the sandwich.

SCRAMBLED EGG/SAUSAGE PATTY/BACON STRIP INTERIOR

C1. Chop 2 pounds of bacon into small pieces.

C2. Fry them inside of a large saucepan and set aside.

C3. Fry the sausages and chop them into small pieces.

C4. In medium bowl, beat all the eggs.

C5. In a large bowl, combine the beaten eggs, sausages, and bacon bits.

C6. Using the large frying pan, cook the entire mixture together creating one consistency.

BUILDING

D1. Take the sausage and cheese out of each of the Sausage McMuffins and set aside.

D2. Lay down one of the egg sandwich pockets.

D3. Put the entire contents of the scrambled egg/bacon/sausage mixture on top.

D4. Cover the eggs with shredded cheese.

D5. Cover the egg contents with half the amount of bacon strips.

D6. Finish the inside with the remaining sausage and cheese patties.

D7. Finish the sandwich by adding the second egg sandwich pocket.

D8. Cut open and enjoy.

Step A2

Step B4

Step D4

FAST FOOD MEAT LOAF

INGREDIENTS

4 pounds bacon

1 cup chopped onion

3 cloves garlic, chopped

5 cups whiskey

4 cups ketchup (entire bottle for other recipe)

1 cup vinegar

3–4 pounds ground beef (depending on the size of your roasting pan)

4 eggs

1 cup bread crumbs

5–6 Big Macs (depending the size of your roasting dish)

SERVES: *3 men or 12 women*

👤👤👤👤👤👤👤👤👤👤👤👤👤👤👤

TOTAL CALORIES

3 4 0 6 5

When we made this recipe, we didn't think it would turn out perfectly intact with the burgers still in the meat, plus it was amazingly delicious.

EQUIPMENT

1 large mixing bowl

1 medium to large saucepan

1 large roasting pan

1 large baking tray

Tinfoil

DIRECTIONS

BACON STRIPS

A1. Preheat the oven to 385°F.

A2. Line cookie sheets with the bacon strips.

A3. Flip and degrease every 10 minutes until the strips have become the consistency you like.

WHISKEY MEAT LOAF SAUCE

B1. Combine onion, garlic, and whiskey in a medium to large saucepan.

B2. Cook the onions and garlic until translucent (about 10 to 20 minutes).

B3. Add ½ cup ketchup and vinegar.

B4. Simmer uncovered until reduced and thickened, about 15 to 25 minutes.

B5. Add more whiskey if a stronger flavor is desired.

GROUND BEEF CASING

C1. Combine ground beef, eggs, remaining ketchup, and bread crumbs in a large mixing bowl.

C2. Mix until there is one consistency.

C3. Line roasting pan with 1-inch-thick base and walls.

C4. On a large baking tray, lay out a 1-inch-thick ground beef ceiling.

C5. Poke a hole in the top and try to press out all the air out of the loaf.

Step B4

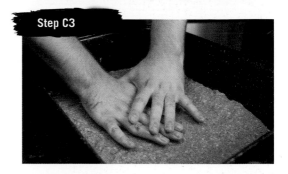

Step C3

Step C4

WHAT YOUR MOM KNOWS

The WWE's World Championship Belt is closely modeled after Muscles Glasses' own World Championship Belt.

BUILDING
MEAT LOAF

Preheat the oven to 400°F.

D1. Line the interior bottom of the meat-lined roasting pan with enough bacon strips to cover the entire floor of the loaf.

D2. Add as many Big Macs as you can fit.

D3. Before closing the meat loaf, cover the top of the Big Macs with more bacon strips.

D4. Turn over the baking tray of ground beef so that it falls onto the top of the loaf, closing the entire thing.

D5. Using your hands, tuck the top of the meat loaf to the base so that it seals in the entire structure.

D6. Cover the meat loaf with tinfoil and bake for 30 minutes.

D7. Take meat loaf out of the oven and drain the grease.

D8. Let it sit for 15 minutes and then turn the meat loaf onto a baking tray (be cautious of the heat).

D9. Pour the whiskey sauce over the entire meat loaf and put it back in the oven for 10 minutes.

Take out and enjoy.

CANDY PIZZA

INGREDIENTS

2 pounds bacon

½ cup cinnamon

1 cup brown sugar

4 tubes cinnamon rolls

4 tubes cookie dough

Various chocolate bars for inside of cookie dough calzone

1 liter corn oil

+ Oh Henry! bars

1 32-ounce box instant pancake mix

4 cups cherries jubilee filling

4 packs cotton candy

+ Various sour candies: gay bacon strips, sour worms, sour rings, and any other candies that simulate pizza toppings

SERVES: *6 humans, no diabetics.*

TOTAL CALORIES
4 2 7 7 5

IF YOU DON'T KNOW, NOW YOU KNOW

We stuffed the cinnamon roll crust with candy bacon, which on its own is a delicious snack.

EQUIPMENT

1 large saucepan

1 large nonstick circular baking sheet

1 rolling pin or cylindrical bottle of alcohol

1 large mixing bowl

Tinfoil

1 large circular nonstick baking pan

1 heat resistant perforated spoon to extract food from deep fryer

DIRECTIONS

CANDY BACON STRIPS

A1. Preheat the oven to 385°F.

A2. Line cookie sheets with the bacon strips.

A3. Mix together the cinnamon and brown sugar and apply it to one side of the strips.

A4. Flip and degrease after 10 minutes.

A5. Apply more sugar mix to the bacon and put back in the oven for 10 minutes.

A6. Repeat until you have cooked all the bacon.

CANDY BACON–STUFFED CINNAMON ROLL PIZZA CRUST

B1. Preheat the oven to 375°F.

B2. Unwrap all the cinnamon roll pieces.

B3. Combine them all together and, using a rolling pin or a cylinder-shaped liquor bottle, roll out pieces into a large circle of dough ¼ of an inch thick.

B4. Line the perimeter of the cinnamon roll dough with the candy bacon strips.

B5. Carefully flip over the dough, creating a stuffed crust.

B6. Bake for 30 minutes.

COOKIE DOUGH CHOCOLATE BAR CALZONE

C1. Leave oven at 375°F.

C2. Combine all the cookie dough together and then cut lump in half.

C3. Using half the amount of cookie dough, roll out a half-circle onto the circular baking sheet.

C4. Lay the chocolate bars onto the base of the half circle, leaving an inch perimeter surrounding them.

C5. Roll out the second half-circle and apply it to the top of the chocolate bars.

C6. Using a fork, press down the edges, sealing the calzone.

C7. Bake in the oven for 20 minutes or until the cookie is golden brown.

OH HENRY! BREAD STICKS

D1. Heat liter of cooking oil in large saucepan until it reaches 395°F.

D2. Put the Oh Henry! bars in the freezer for 20 minutes.

D3. In the meantime, make your instant pancake batter.

D4. Dip the frozen bars in the pancake batter until it has coated them.

D5. Deep fry for 2 minutes, or until the dough has become golden brown.

Step B3

Step B4

Step E2

Step E3

WHAT YOUR MOM KNOWS

Deep-fried chocolate bars used to give me pimples.

BUILDING

E1. When the cinnamon roll pizza dough is done cooking, set aside and let it cool.

E2. Start building the pizza by putting on the cherries jubilee spread as pizza sauce.

E3. Use the cotton candy as cheese and then proceed to apply all the candies on top as pizza toppings.

BaconStrips&
BaconStrips&
BaconStrips&
BaconStrips&
BaconStrips